THE ANCIENT ROMANS

by Elizabeth Andrews

DiscoverRoo
An Imprint of Pop!
popbooksonline.com

WELCOME TO DiscoverRoo!

This book is filled with videos, puzzles, games, and more! Scan the QR codes* while you read, or visit the website below to make this book pop.

popbooksonline.com/anc-romans

abdobooks.com

Published by Pop!, a division of ABDO, PO Box 398166, Minneapolis, Minnesota 55439. Copyright © 2023 by Abdo Consulting Group, Inc. International copyrights reserved in all countries. No part of this book may be reproduced in any form without written permission from the publisher. DiscoverRoo™ is a trademark and logo of Pop!.

Printed in the United States of America, North Mankato, Minnesota.

102022
012023

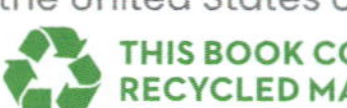
THIS BOOK CONTAINS RECYCLED MATERIALS

Cover Photo: Fototeca Storica Nazionale/Getty Images, Shutterstock Images

Interior Photos: Shutterstock Images, Wikimedia Commons, Kharbine-Tapabor/Shutterstock, Design Pics Inc/Shutterstock, Historia/Shutterstock, Farnese Collection, Palace Bevilacqua in Verona, Jane Taylor/Shutterstock,

Editor: Emily Dreher

Series Designer: Laura Graphenteen

Library of Congress Control Number: 2022941121

Publisher's Cataloging-in-Publication Data

Names: Andrews, Elizabeth, author.

Title: The ancient Romans / by Elizabeth Andrews

Description: Minneapolis, Minnesota : Pop!, 2023 | Series: Ancient civilizations | Includes online resources and index.

Identifiers: ISBN 9781098243265 (lib. bdg.) | ISBN 9781098243968 (ebook)

Subjects: LCSH: Italy--History--Juvenile literature. | Romans--Juvenile literature. | Ancient civilization--Juvenile literature. | Indigenous peoples--Social life and customs--Juvenile literature. | Cultural anthropology--Juvenile literature.

Classification: DDC 972.01--dc23

*Scanning QR codes requires a web-enabled smart device with a QR code reader app and a camera.

TABLE OF CONTENTS

CHAPTER 1

VENI, VIDI, VICI

Ancient Rome was the first civilization to bring together the western world. At its height of power, Rome ruled 60 million people across millions of miles. In 1000 BCE, it began as a region along the Tiber River south of modern-day Rome called

Ruins of the Roman Forum still stand. It was the center of business, government, and socializing.

Latium. The people were divided in two groups: the Latins and the Etruscans. They were ruled by an Etruscan **monarchy**.

Hospitals began on Roman battlefields. Doctors traveled with armies to help the wounded.

Within 400 years, Latium had roads.
The roads allowed Rome, Latium's largest
village, to trade with neighbors. A city
center and cattle market were also built.
In 509 BCE, the Latins overthrew the
Etruscan monarchy.

Rome became a walled **city-state**.
It was the most powerful city-state in
central Italy. Rome successfully **invaded**
neighboring city-states.

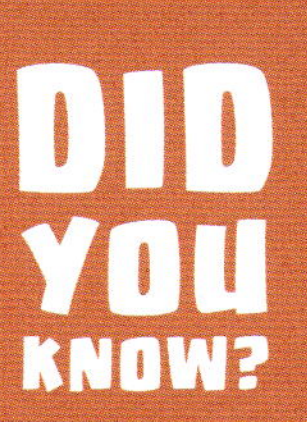

Veni, vidi, vici means "I came,
I saw, I **conquered**." It is a
popular phrase from ancient
Rome about all the victories the
Romans had.

Rome spread past central Italy. By 200 BCE, it had conquered the Italian **peninsula**. This connected Rome to the Mediterranean Sea. At this point, Rome had a powerful army. It took land from almost everyone it battled. The Punic Wars started in 264 BCE and lasted more than 100 years. Winning these wars gave Rome rule in northern Africa and Spain.

Romans took home treasures from the places they invaded. The ancient Romans conquered everywhere from the modern-day British Isles to the

Middle East. Expansion lasted until 117 CE.

However, the empire was stretched

thin. Armies became more loyal to

commanders than to their emperor.

People in conquered lands started

fighting for their freedom.

CHAPTER 2

ROMAN GOVERNMENT

In 509 BCE, Romans overthrew the Etruscan **monarchy**. Then they made a new government called the Roman Republic. A republic puts power in the people's hands. The government was led by elected senators. They decided

how Rome would be organized and run. Senators passed laws and chose where the army would **invade** next.

The Roman Republic inspired the United States' government structure.

The ancient Romans were divided
into different groups. The patricians were
rich, property-owning men. The plebeians
were commoners, like farmers, bakers,
and builders.

It was common for senators to fight and disagree.

At the start of the Roman Republic, only patricians could vote for senators. They were also the only people who could be senators. In 367 BCE, plebeians got the right to vote and hold office. Plebeian court officials were called tribunes.

But patricians still had the most power. They got richer as Rome expanded. The poor knew this was unfair. The inequalities lead to war. A group of three army generals quickly gained power during the unrest. One of these generals was **notorious** Julius Caesar.

The senate did not like Caesar. He was gaining too much power, and he had a whole army supporting him. Caesar declared himself the single ruler of Rome in 45 BCE. He was killed by senators the next year.

Before his death, Caesar declared his adopted son, Octavian, his **heir**. Octavian

The senators who killed Caesar ran through the streets to celebrate his death.

and Caesar's closest ally, Mark Antony, decided to split Rome between them. They also defeated the senators who killed Caesar. Ten years later, Octavian decided he wanted to rule Rome on his own. He went to war against Antony and won. In 27 BCE, Octavian became the first emperor of Rome and earned the new name Augustus, meaning "the **revered** one."

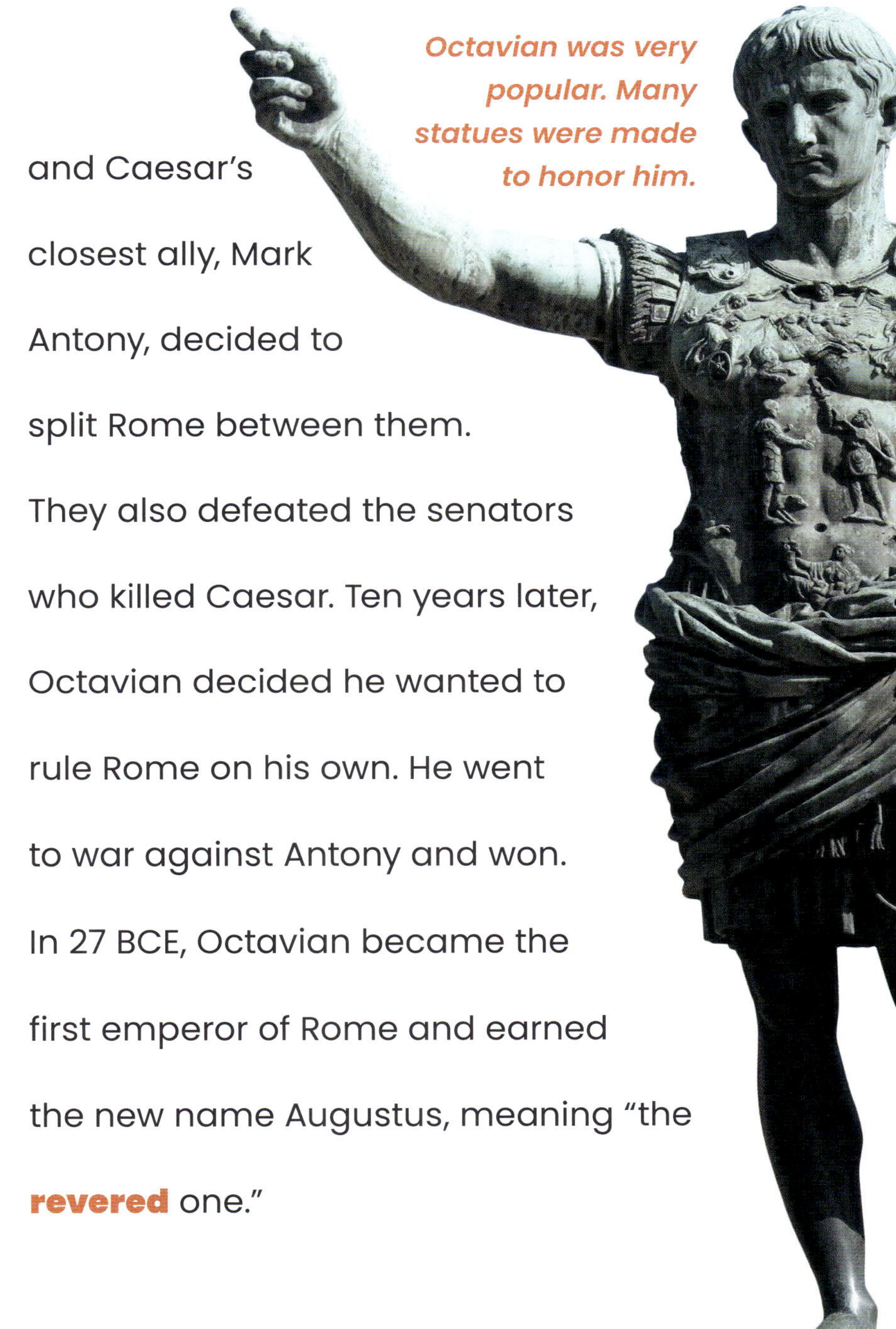

TIMELINE OF ROMAN EMPERORS

Augustus (Octavian) (31 BCE–14 CE)

First Roman Emperor

Claudius (41–54 CE)

Expanded Roman Empire into Britain and Northern Africa

Trajan (98–117 CE)

Ruled 60 million people when Rome was at its height of power

Augustus took power from the senate. The Roman Republic became the Roman Empire. The senate still had a voice, but decisions could be **vetoed** by the emperor. He had total power over the

Arcadius
(383–402 CE)

Honorius
(393–423 CE)

Romulus Augustulus
(475–476 CE)

Arcadius (ruled the East) and Honorius (ruled the West) split the Roman Empire in two

Last Western Roman emperor, who was overthrown by a German warrior

army, laws, and who joined the senate.

Rome was led by one emperor until 395 CE. Then it split into the Eastern and Western Roman Empires. The West fell in 476, but the East survived until 1453!

CHAPTER 3

ROMAN GODS AND MAN

People in ancient Rome worshipped gods and goddesses. They made offerings, built beautiful temples, and held festivals to honor their gods. Every Roman city had a temple to the sky-god Jupiter, his wife,

Juno, and Minerva, who was the goddess of wisdom and arts. These three gods made up the *Capitoline Triad.*

Offerings were gifts given to the gods to please them and earn their protection for the empire.

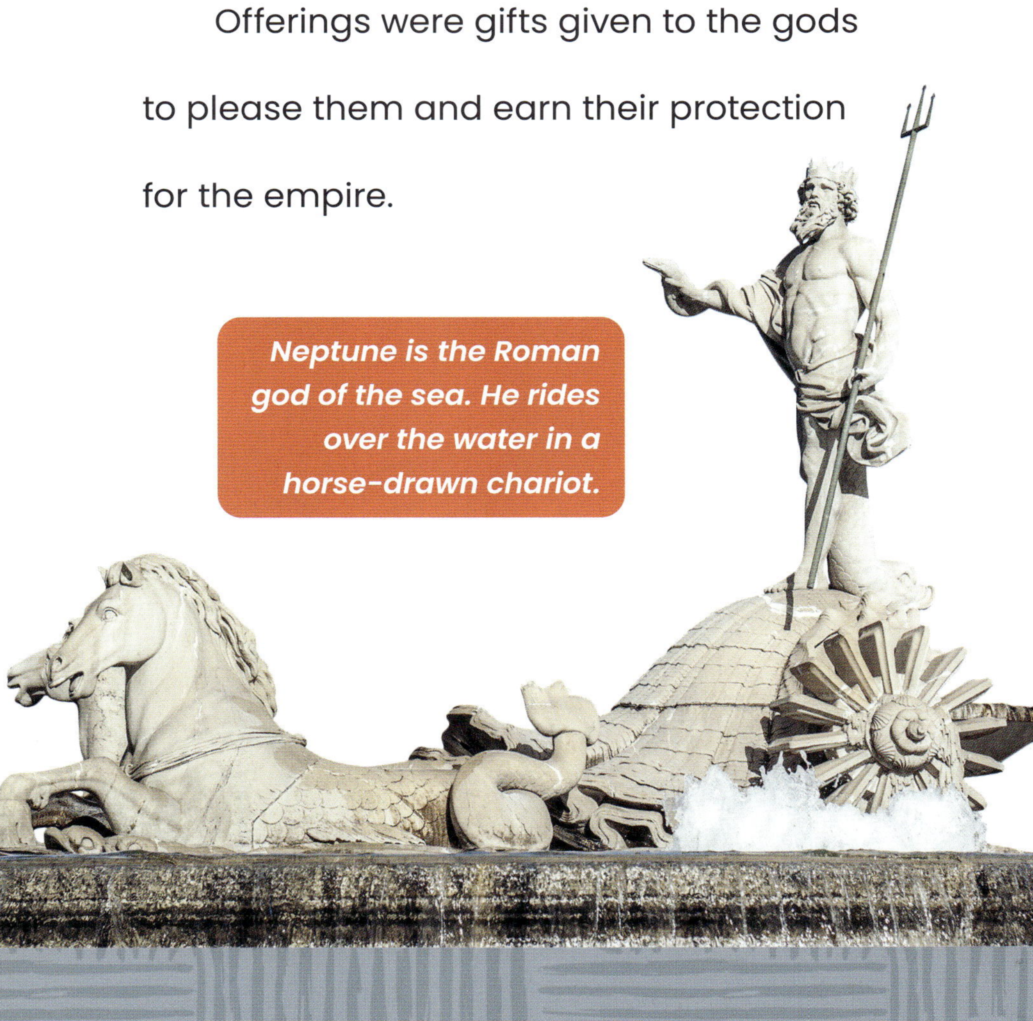

As ancient Rome spread, it

conquered people who followed different

religions. Romans mixed new religions

into their worship. Eventually they came upon other religions with just one god, such as Judaism and Christianity. In 380 CE, Christianity became the official religion of the empire.

Men were the most valued members of Roman society. Only they could vote, own property, and serve as military and government officials. Ordinary men were traders, farmers, builders, or soldiers. Women stayed at home. Some would work as midwives or dressmakers.

Ancient Roman families were led by the oldest living male member. This role was called **paterfamilias**. The father had total power over everyone in the family. Even if a son was an adult and married with his own children, he could not own any property until his father died. The oldest woman ran the household and was

very respected.

THE GLORY OF ROME

Roman art and architecture are world famous. Much has crumbled with time, but precious pieces and places still remain.

People from all over the world travel to Rome to see the Colosseum.

Rich Romans decorated their homes with large, colorful murals and mosaics.

Roman sculptures were much like those of the ancient Greeks. Many famous ancient Roman artists were originally from Greece before it was **conquered** by Rome. Roman sculptures are known for having lifelike facial expressions.

The Colosseum is the most famous landmark of ancient Rome. It was built from concrete and stone with only hand tools. Events, like chariot races and gladiator battles, were held there. Beneath the floor, there were chambers and passages where gladiators and animals lived. The Colosseum has survived earthquakes and lightning strikes.

Gladiators and wild animals, such as tigers, zebras, bears, and elephants, lived and fought in the Colosseum.

The best-preserved building of ancient Rome is the Pantheon. It is a round temple with a big domed roof. Light shines through a 30-foot (9m) window in the center of the dome. The Pantheon has stayed in good shape because it has been continuously used. It has been

A rotunda is a round building covered by a dome.

a temple, shrine, church, and place for famous Italians to be buried.

Ancient Romans were good at planning. They built aqueducts to carry water throughout the empire. They also made sewer systems to move waste out of the cities. Roadways were well-planned and connected the empire. Some are still used today!

For more than 2,000 years, Rome had a strong influence where it ruled. Even after it fell, ancient Rome inspired the Western world for centuries.

MAKING CONNECTIONS

TEXT-TO-SELF

What animals would you have wanted to see at the Colosseum if you lived in ancient Rome?

TEXT-TO-TEXT

Have you read any other books about ancient civilizations? If so, what did they have in common with ancient Rome?

TEXT-TO-WORLD

How do you think the world would be different if ancient Rome never existed?

GLOSSARY

city-state — a state made of a city and its surrounding territory.

conquer — to gain land by force.

heir — a person who receives or has the right to receive another person's property or title after that person's death.

invade — to enter an area by force, in order to conquer.

monarchy — rule by a single person, such as a king or emperor.

notorious — widely known and talked about.

paterfamilias — the father and leader of a family.

peninsula — a piece of land surrounded by water on three sides.

revered — worthy of great honor and respect.

veto — to prevent something from taking effect.

INDEX

popbooksonline.com/anc-romans

*Scanning QR codes requires a web-enabled smart device with a QR code reader app and a camera.